Salt of the Earth, Light of the Word

Empowering Change Through Faith

Somer Lofton

"See the good
in yourself and
in others."

Table of Contents

In a world often fraught with confusion and discord, "Be the Righteous" may serve as a testament to Your eternal principles of justice, compassion, and forgiveness.

Acknowledgment:

This book will catalyze a transformation in your life, akin to its profound impact on mine as I poured research and thoughts into my computer. Your willingness to invest your time and focus on these words is truly valued.

But most importantly, my husband deserves special recognition for his extraordinary patience and unwavering support. He has been instrumental in leading our family as we strive to embody the ideals of being "Salt of the earth and Light of the world," as scripture instructs us in the Gospel of Matthew.

I sincerely thank my children for their strength, understanding, and resilience. They are tiny warriors of God's army, embodying faith and courage beyond their years.

I cannot forget my gratitude for my parents and bonus-parents, whose unwavering support and guidance have shaped me into who I am today. Their love, sacrifice, and encouragement have been the cornerstones of my journey, instilling in me the values of compassion and integrity. I am truly blessed to have been raised by such remarkable people.

May the pages of this
book echo the depth of
Your compassion and the
brilliance of Your truth.

Dear God,

With profound reverence and gratitude, I dedicate my book *Salt of the Earth, Light of the World* to You, the source of all wisdom and love. As I embark on this journey of sharing insights and reflections, I am mindful of Your divine presence guiding every word and thought. May the pages of this book echo the depth of Your compassion and the brilliance of Your truth.

In a world fraught with confusion and discord, *Salt of the Earth, Light of the World* may serve as a testament to Your eternal principles of justice, compassion, and forgiveness. May its message inspire readers to cultivate righteousness in their hearts and actions, to uphold integrity and kindness in all their endeavors.

I offer this humble offering as an expression of my devotion and gratitude for Your boundless blessings and guidance.

"Be the energy
you want to attract".

Prologue

Can we take the time to pause and reflect? By reflecting we may realize that our choices and our actions hold the power to enrich the lives of others. Imagine for a moment that, just as salt enhances the taste of our food, our lives should enhance the spiritual flavor of the lives around us. But, like most things, there is a catch—if we prioritize our gain over the process set by God, we miss fulfilling our life's purpose. We must resist staying in comfort and convenience because we must obey the guidance of God.

As we embark on this journey of faith, let us heed the words of Jesus, who declared, "You are the salt of the earth. But if the salt loses its saltiness, how can it be made salty again? It is no longer good for anything, except to be thrown out and trampled by men." Let us embrace our role as Salt and Light with boldness and conviction, knowing that, through us, God's love will shine forth, illuminating the darkness and transforming hearts and lives for eternity.

So, the call to transformation is a sacred invitation to embrace God's saving grace and allow his love to permeate every area of our lives. Through prayer, meditation, and spiritual guidance, we open ourselves to the transformative work of the Holy Spirit, who molds us into vessels of God's grace and instruments of his peace.

As we journey along this path of transformation, may we shine forth as beacons of hope and redemption, illuminating the darkness and pointing others to the love and mercy of our Savior, Jesus Christ?

Ultimately, being Salt and Light is not merely a metaphorical concept but a call to action for believers everywhere. It is a call to live lives of integrity and righteousness, demonstrating compassion and empathy toward those in need, speaking out against injustice and oppression, and sharing the message of God's love and salvation with a world in desperate need of hope. As we embrace this call and allow God's love to flow through us, we can make a tangible impact on the world around us, illuminating the darkness and pointing others toward the light of Christ.

Fulfilling our hunger for righteousness is a lifelong journey that requires intentionality, discipline, and a willingness to seek God with our whole hearts. Through prayer, fellowship, and studying God's word, we deepen our connection with God and nourish our souls with the goodness of his love. And as we live lives that reflect God's love and goodness, we bring honor and glory to his name, fulfilling our purpose as his disciples in the world.

Let's commit to shining brightly as Salt and Light in our communities. Let's intentionally extend kindness, show compassion, and spread positivity wherever we go. By embodying these principles in our daily lives, we can make a difference in the lives of those around us and be agents of transformation in a world that desperately needs it. As Matthew 5:16 says, "In the same way, let your light shine before others, that they may see your good deeds and glorify your Father in heaven." Let's illuminate the path forward with hope, love, and the transformative power of Christ's love.

Let's commit to shining
brightly as Salt and
Light in our
communities.

Chapter 1: Embracing Our Role

Have you ever contemplated your role as a Christian in this world? Is it akin to being Salt and Light? Can we add flavor and brightness to the lives around us? These questions stir the depths of our souls, prompting us to delve into the essence of our faith and purpose. As we embark on this journey of exploration, let us first grasp the significance of being Salt and Light in a world that often succumbs to darkness.

Two million years ago, in the land of Nazareth, Jesus Christ walked among humanity, his teachings resonating with truth and compassion. Born into humble beginnings, his life unfolded as a testament to love, service, and redemption. Through his words and actions, he gathered disciples, kindling a fire of faith that would illuminate the path for generations to come.

Yet, as the shadows of opposition grew darker, Jesus faced false accusations and condemnation by the religious authorities in Jerusalem. His crucifixion by Roman rulers marked the climax of his earthly journey, but it was not the end. Even in death, his disciples carried forth his message, spreading the gospel everywhere, igniting hearts with the flame of salvation.

Jesus's life and mission were extraordinary, marked by miraculous healings that brought sight to the blind and solace to the suffering. His acceptance of the marginalized—from the outcast to the oppressed—spoke volumes about the boundless reach of his love. In his warm embrace, children found sanctuary, their innocence cherished, and their spirits uplifted.

However, the most profound testament to Jesus's embodiment of Salt and Light was his act of forgiveness. Even as nails pierced his flesh and agony seared his soul, he uttered words of grace and mercy, extending forgiveness to those who sought his demise. In that moment, he epitomized the essence of Salt and Light, infusing the world with the transformative power of divine love.

As followers of Christ, we are called to emulate his example, to embrace our role as Salt and Light in a world hungering for hope and redemption. Just as salt enhances flavor and light dispels darkness, so too are we tasked with enriching the lives of those around us, illuminating the path to truth and righteousness.

Our journey as Salt and Light begins with introspection and self-awareness. We must first examine our hearts and minds, seeking to align our thoughts and actions with the teachings of Jesus Christ. Are we living lives of integrity, compassion, and humility? Are we demonstrating love and kindness to our neighbors, both near and far? These questions compel us to consider the authenticity of our faith and the sincerity of our devotion.

But being Salt and Light extends beyond mere introspection; it requires active engagement with the world around us. We are called to be agents of change, catalysts for transformation, and advocates for justice. Whether it be through acts of service, advocacy for the marginalized, or speaking out against oppression, we have a responsibility to make a positive impact on society.

Moreover, being Salt and Light necessitates a willingness to step out of our comfort zones and embrace the unknown. It requires courage to confront injustice, humility to admit our shortcomings, and perseverance to endure in the face of adversity. Yet, it is through these trials and tribulations that our faith is strengthened, and our character refined.

In our pursuit of being Salt and Light, we must also cultivate a spirit of unity and collaboration within the body of Christ. Just as each grain of salt contributes to the overall flavor of a dish, and each ray of light combines to illuminate the darkness, so too are we called to work together in harmony and solidarity. Regardless of denominational differences or theological disagreements, we are united by our shared commitment to follow Jesus Christ and spread his message of love and redemption.

As we navigate the complexities of life, let us never lose sight of the transformative power of being Salt and Light. In our words and deeds, may we reflect the love and grace of our Heavenly Father, bringing healing to the broken, hope to the despairing, and light to those lost in darkness. Let us be unyielding in our pursuit of righteousness, unwavering in our commitment to justice, and unrelenting in our proclamation of the Good News.

The call to be Salt and Light is not merely a metaphorical concept, but a sacred duty entrusted to every follower of Christ. It is a call to embody the teachings of Jesus Christ in our daily lives, to be vessels of his love and instruments of his peace. As we embark on this journey of faith, let us heed the words of Jesus, who declared, "You are the salt of the earth . . . You are the light of the world." (Matthew 5:13–14) May we embrace our role with humility and gratitude, knowing that through us, God's love will shine forth, illuminating the darkness and transforming hearts and lives for eternity.

The journey of
transformation begins with a
humble acknowledgment of
our need for God's grace.

Chapter 2: The Call to Transformation

Being Salt and Light is not merely a title bestowed upon us as followers of Christ; it is a call to undergo a profound transformation of heart and soul. This transformation, ignited by embracing God's saving grace, is not a one-time event but a continuous journey of renewal and growth. As we delve into the depths of this transformative process, we come to understand the essence of our role as Salt and Light in a world hungering for hope and redemption.

The journey of transformation begins with a humble acknowledgment of our need for God's grace. It is through this grace that our hearts are softened, our spirits renewed, and our minds transformed. Just as a seed requires nourishment to blossom into a mighty oak, so too do we require the nurturing touch of God's love to flourish into vessels of his grace.

Prayer becomes our lifeline, a sacred communion with the divine that nourishes our souls and guides our steps. In the quiet moments of solitude, we lay bare our fears, doubts, and struggles before the throne of grace, trusting in God's unfailing love and mercy. Through prayer, we invite God's presence to dwell within us, shaping us into vessels of his grace and instruments of his peace.

Meditation becomes our practice, a disciplined reflection on God's word and his wondrous works. In the stillness of our hearts, we ponder the mysteries of faith, allowing the truth of Scripture to penetrate our minds and hearts. As we meditate on God's promises and his faithfulness throughout history, we are reminded of his unchanging love and his sovereign control over all things.

Fasting becomes our discipline, a voluntary denial of physical sustenance to nourish our spiritual hunger. In abstaining from food, we humble ourselves before God, acknowledging our dependence on him for sustenance and strength. Through fasting, we cultivate a deeper intimacy with God, drawing closer to him and aligning our desires with his will.

Service becomes our mission, a selfless outpouring of love and compassion toward others. In serving the least of these, we emulate the example of Christ, who came not to be served, but to serve. Whether it be feeding the hungry, clothing the naked, or caring for the sick, our acts of service bear witness to the transformative power of God's love at work in the world.

Suffering becomes our teacher, a refining fire that purifies our faith and strengthens our resolve. Amid trials and tribulations, we cling to the hope of glory, knowing that our present sufferings are but a prelude to the eternal weight of glory that awaits us. As we endure hardships with patience and perseverance, we are conformed evermore to the image of Christ, who suffered on our behalf.

Community becomes our support, a fellowship of believers united in faith and love. In the company of fellow pilgrims, we find encouragement, accountability, and mutual edification. Together, we share in each other's joys and sorrows, bearing one another's burdens and spurring one another toward love and honorable deeds.

As we journey deeper into the transformative process of becoming Salt and Light, we are confronted with the reality of our brokenness and inadequacy. We recognize that apart from Christ, we can do nothing and that our sufficiency comes from God alone. Yet, in our weakness, God's strength is made perfect, and his grace is sufficient for all our needs.

The journey of transformation is not without its challenges and obstacles. We will encounter times of doubt, fear, and temptation along the way. Yet, we press on, knowing that the God who began a good work in us will bring it to completion on the day of Christ Jesus. With our eyes fixed on Jesus, the author, and perfecter of our faith, we run the race set before us with endurance, laying aside every weight and sin that clings so closely.

Ultimately, the journey of transformation leads us to a deeper intimacy with God and a greater conformity to the image of Christ. As we abide in Christ, we bear fruit that remains, bringing glory to God and blessing to others. Our lives become a living testimony to the transformative power of God's grace, as we reflect his love and light to a world in need.

The journey of transformation as Salt and Light is a lifelong process of surrender, obedience, and faithfulness. It requires us to continually yield to the work of the Holy Spirit in our lives, allowing him to mold us and shape us into the image of Christ. As we abide in Christ and walk in obedience to his word, we become increasingly effective as agents of God's kingdom, bringing hope, healing, and redemption to a broken and hurting world. May we embrace this journey with humility and perseverance, knowing that God, who called us, is faithful, and he will surely accomplish his purposes in and through us.

Matthew 5, Jesus explicitly calls his followers the "salt of the earth" and the "light of the world," urging them not to lose their distinctiveness

Chapter 3: Salt and Light in Action

When we speak of being Salt and Light, it transcends mere seasoning and illumination. These metaphors hold profound significance, rooted in the teachings of Scripture and the life example of Jesus Christ. Salt, as symbolized in Leviticus, signifies purity and the covenant between God and his people. It serves as a reminder of our faithfulness and commitment to God's divine plan. Similarly, the metaphor of light in Proverbs contrasts the righteous, who illuminate the path of goodness, with the wicked, whose actions lead to darkness and ruin.

In Matthew 5, Jesus explicitly calls his followers the "salt of the earth" and the "light of the world," urging them not to lose their distinctiveness. These metaphors, deeply ingrained in the cultural context of Jesus's time, hold timeless truths that resonate with believers today. Salt, in ancient times, was not merely a seasoning but a preservative, essential for preserving food in a world without modern refrigeration. In the same way, believers are called to preserve goodness in a world marred by sin and corruption. Our presence should act as a counterbalance to the moral decay that threatens to engulf society.

Likewise, light symbolizes the transformative power of God's truth, guiding others toward righteousness through righteous actions. Just as a lamp dispels darkness, so too do believers illuminate the path for others to follow. Our lives should reflect the radiance of God's love, shining brightly in a world desperately in need of hope and redemption.

But how do we embody Salt and Light in our daily lives? How do we put these metaphors into action and make a tangible impact on the world around us? The answer lies in our willingness to live out our faith with boldness and conviction, allowing God's love to flow through us and touch the lives of those we encounter.

One way we can be Salt and Light is by living lives of integrity and righteousness. In a world plagued by moral relativism and ethical compromise, our commitment to truth and goodness stands as a beacon of hope. Whether in our workplaces, our communities, or our homes, we should strive to uphold the highest standards of ethical conduct, refusing to succumb to the forcing of peer pressure or societal norms.

Another way we can be Salt and Light is by demonstrating compassion and empathy toward those in need. Jesus himself was known for his compassion toward the marginalized and oppressed, reaching out to the outcasts of society with love and acceptance. As his followers, we are called to follow him, extending a helping hand to the poor, the sick, and the downtrodden. Whether through acts of service, financial assistance, or simply a listening ear, we can make a difference in the lives of those who are suffering.

Additionally, we can be Salt and Light by speaking out against injustice and oppression wherever we encounter it. Jesus was a vocal advocate for the marginalized and oppressed, challenging the religious and political authorities of his time to uphold the principles of justice and equality. As his followers, we are called to do the same, standing up for the rights of the oppressed and working to bring about positive change in our communities and beyond.

Furthermore, we can be Salt and Light by sharing the message of God's love and salvation with those who have yet to experience it. Just as salt enhances the flavor of food, so can our words and actions enhance the spiritual lives of those around us. Whether through personal evangelism, outreach ministries, or simply living out our faith authentically, we can point others toward the source of sincere hope and fulfillment.

But the most important aspect of being Salt and Light is to do so with humility and grace. We are called to be salt and light not for our glory or recognition, but to bring glory to God and to draw others closer to him. Our actions should reflect the love and compassion of Christ, leading others to see the beauty of the gospel lived out in our lives.

Ultimately, being Salt and Light is not merely a metaphorical concept but a call to action for believers everywhere. It is a call to live lives of integrity and righteousness, demonstrating compassion and empathy toward those in need, speaking out against injustice and oppression, and sharing the message of God's love and salvation with a world in desperate need of hope. As we embrace this call and allow God's love to flow through us, we can make a tangible impact on the world around us, illuminating the darkness and pointing others toward the light of Christ.

But how do we uphold our role as Salt and Light in a world that often values conformity over conviction, comfort over sacrifice?

Chapter 4: Upholding Our Role

Maintaining our role as Salt and Light in a world often characterized by darkness and decay requires an unwavering commitment to Christ's teachings and values. It demands steadfast adherence to the principles of truth, righteousness, and love, even in the face of opposition or persecution. Any deviation toward worldly comforts or pursuits risks compromising our distinctiveness and effectiveness in influencing society. As followers of Christ, we are called to be *in* the world but not *of* the world—to stand apart from the prevailing culture and embody a counter-cultural witness that reflects the transformative power of the Gospel.

In Matthew 5:13, Jesus exhorts his followers, "You are the salt of the earth. But if the salt loses its saltiness, how can it be made salty again? It is no longer good for anything, except to be thrown out and trampled by men." This metaphor underscores the importance of maintaining our distinctiveness as followers of Christ. Just as salt preserves and enhances flavor, so too are we called to preserve and enhance the moral fabric of society through our words and actions. However, if we lose sight of our identity and compromise our values for the sake of worldly gain or acceptance, we risk becoming ineffective in fulfilling our role as agents of positive change.

Similarly, in Matthew 5:14–16, Jesus declares, "You are the light of the world. A town built on a hill cannot be hidden. Neither do people light a lamp and put it under a bowl. Instead, they put it on its stand, and it gives light to everyone in the house. In the same way, let your light shine before others, that they may see your good deeds and glorify your Father in heaven." Here, Jesus emphasizes the importance of shining brightly as beacons of truth and righteousness in a world shrouded in darkness. Our lives should reflect the radiance of God's love, illuminating the path for others to follow and drawing them closer to the source of all light: Jesus Christ.

But how do we uphold our role as Salt and Light in a world that often values conformity over conviction, comfort over sacrifice? The answer lies in our unwavering commitment to Christ and his teachings, even when it requires us to swim against the cultural tide. It means living lives of integrity and moral courage, refusing to compromise our principles for the sake of popularity or acceptance.

One way we can uphold our role as Salt and Light is by maintaining a fervent devotion to prayer and spiritual disciplines. Prayer serves as a lifeline to the divine, a source of strength and guidance in life's challenges and temptations. Through prayer, we cultivate a deep intimacy with God and align our hearts with his will, enabling us to withstand the pressures of the world and remain steadfast in our commitment to righteousness.

Another way we can uphold our role is by actively seeking opportunities to engage with and influence the culture around us. Whether through our vocations, our relationships, or our involvement in the community, we should strive to be salt and light in every sphere of life. This may involve speaking out against injustice, advocating for the marginalized, or simply living out our faith authentically in the public square. By doing so, we can make a tangible impact on the world around us and contribute to the advancement of God's kingdom on earth.

Furthermore, we can uphold our role by fostering unity and harmony within the body of Christ. As Mark 9:50 reminds us, "Salt is good, but if it loses its saltiness, how can you make it salty again? Have salt among yourselves and be at peace with each other." Maintaining peace and harmony among believers is essential to retaining our effectiveness as Salt and Light in the world. When we allow division and discord to prevail among us, we undermine our witness and diminish our impact on society. Therefore, we must strive to cultivate a spirit of unity and mutual respect within the body of Christ, recognizing that our strength lies in our solidarity and our ability to bear witness to the transforming power of God's love.

Ultimately, being Salt and Light is not merely a metaphorical concept but a call to action for believers everywhere. It is a call to live lives of integrity and righteousness, demonstrating compassion and empathy toward those in need, speaking out against injustice and oppression, and sharing the message of God's love and salvation with a world in desperate need of hope. As we embrace this call and allow God's love to flow through us, we can make a tangible impact on the world around us, illuminating the darkness and pointing others toward the light of Christ.

At the core of our role as
Salt and Light is
righteousness, a
foundational principle
that guides our thoughts,
words, and actions.

Chapter 5: The Essence of Righteousness

At the core of our role as Salt and Light is righteousness, a foundational principle that guides our thoughts, words, and actions. Righteousness encompasses a deep-seated commitment to goodness, justice, and virtue, rooted in our relationship with God and our love for humanity. It reflects God's character and is a testament to our transformation through Christ.

But what does righteousness truly entail, and how does it manifest in our lives as followers of Christ? Righteousness is more than just adhering to a set of moral codes or religious rituals; it is a way of being, a disposition of the heart that seeks to honor God in all things. As Jesus teaches in Matthew 6:1, "Be careful not to practice your righteousness in front of others to be seen by them. If you do, you will have no reward from your Father in heaven." Righteousness is not about seeking praise or recognition from others but about living in alignment with God's will and serving others selflessly.

One aspect of righteousness is standing against injustice and oppression wherever it may be found. Throughout the Bible, we see countless examples of God's people speaking out against injustice and advocating for the marginalized. From the prophets of the Old Testament to the early Christian church, followers of God have been called to be voices for the voiceless and champions for the oppressed. As it says in Proverbs 31:8–9, "Speak up for those who cannot speak for themselves, for the rights of all who are destitute. Speak up and judge fairly; defend the rights of the poor and needy." Righteousness compels us to confront systems of oppression and work toward a more just and equitable society.

Furthermore, righteousness involves actively seeking to positively impact the world around us. It means using our time, talents, and resources to uplift others and spread kindness and compassion wherever we go. As it says in Galatians 6:9–10, "Let us not become weary in doing good, for at the proper time we will reap a harvest if we do not give up. Therefore, as we have the opportunity, let us do good to all people, especially to those who belong to the family of believers." Righteousness is about being proactive in our pursuit of justice and mercy, recognizing that even the smallest acts of kindness can have a profound impact on those around us.

Moreover, righteousness is characterized by humility and a recognition of our limitations. As it says in Romans 3:23, "For all have sinned and fall short of the glory of God." None of us are perfect, and righteousness does not mean that we will never make mistakes or fall short of God's standards. Rather, righteousness involves acknowledging our weaknesses and relying on God's grace to guide us in our journey toward holiness. It is a continual process of growth and transformation, fueled by our desire to become more like Christ.

In addition, righteousness is marked by a commitment to truth and integrity in all aspects of our lives. As it says in Ephesians 4:25, "Therefore each of you must put off falsehood and speak truthfully to your neighbor, for we are all members of one body." Righteousness requires us to be honest and transparent in our dealings with others, to speak the truth in love, and to uphold the highest ethical standards in our personal and professional lives. It means living with integrity and authenticity, even when it is difficult or unpopular to do so.

Furthermore, righteousness is characterized by a spirit of generosity and compassion toward those in need. As it says in Proverbs 19:17, "Whoever is kind to the poor lends to the Lord, and he will reward them for what they have done." Righteousness compels us to care for the marginalized, the oppressed, and the vulnerable, to extend a helping hand to those in need, and to share our blessings with others generously. It reflects God's compassion toward us and is a tangible expression of our love for our neighbors.

Righteousness is not merely a set of rules to be followed or a list of deeds to be checked off; it is a way of life, a posture of the heart that seeks to honor God in all things. It is about living with integrity and authenticity, standing against injustice, and spreading kindness and compassion wherever we go. As followers of Christ, may we strive to embody the essence of righteousness in our lives, allowing our actions to reflect God's love and grace to a world in need of hope and healing.

Kindness is characterized
by honesty, the
cornerstone of
truthfulness and integrity.

Chapter 6: The Ripple Effect of Kindness

Kindness and a loving spirit are not merely virtues to be admired from afar but principles to be actively practiced and embraced in our daily lives. They hold the power to transform not only our interactions but also the world around us, creating a ripple effect of positivity and compassion that touches the lives of countless others.

At the heart of kindness lies empathy, the ability to understand and share the feelings of others. Empathy is more than just a fleeting emotion; it is a deep-seated understanding of human experience and a willingness to connect with others on a profound level. When we approach life with empathy, we become attuned to the needs and struggles of those around us, offering a listening ear, a comforting presence, and a helping hand to those who need it most. As it says in Romans 12:15, "Rejoice with those who rejoice, weep with those who weep." Empathy allows us to walk alongside others in both their joys and their sorrows, sharing their experiences and offering support and encouragement along the way.

Kindness is characterized by honesty, the cornerstone of truthfulness and integrity. Honesty means speaking the truth in love, even when it is difficult or uncomfortable to do so. It involves owning up to our mistakes, admitting when we are wrong, and striving to live with authenticity and transparency in all aspects of our lives. As it says in Ephesians 4:25, "Therefore each of you must put off falsehood and speak truthfully to your neighbor, for we are all members of one body." Honesty fosters trust and respect in our relationships, allowing us to build deeper connections with others based on mutual understanding and transparency.

Furthermore, kindness requires courage, the willingness to step out of our comfort zones and stand up for what is right. Courage is not the absence of fear but the ability to act despite it, to confront injustice, and to advocate for change even in the face of opposition or adversity. As it says in Joshua 1:9, "Be strong and courageous. Do not be afraid; do not be discouraged, for the Lord your God will be with you wherever you go." Courage empowers us to speak out against oppression, to defend the rights of the marginalized, and to work toward a more just and equitable society. It is a testament to our commitment to righteousness and justice, even when it requires us to make sacrifices or face opposition from others.

Moreover, kindness and a loving spirit have a ripple effect that extends far beyond our actions, touching the lives of countless others in ways we may never fully realize. When we show kindness to others, it has a way of spreading like wildfire, inspiring others to pay it forward, and creating a chain reaction of compassion and generosity. As it says in Luke 6:38, "Give, and it will be given to you. A good measure, pressed down, shaken together, and running over, will be poured into your lap. For with the measure you use, it will be measured to you." Kindness begets kindness, and the more we give of ourselves to others, the more blessings we receive in return.

Furthermore, kindness and a loving spirit have the power to break down barriers and bridge divides, uniting people from diverse backgrounds and perspectives in a spirit of unity and mutual respect. When we approach others with kindness and compassion, we create an atmosphere of acceptance and understanding where all are welcome and valued for who they are. As it says in Colossians 3:14, "And over all these virtues put on love, which binds them all together in perfect unity." Love is the ultimate expression of kindness, transcending differences and bringing people together in a spirit of harmony and cooperation.

Kindness and a loving spirit are not just nice ideals to aspire to but essential components of our identity as followers of Christ. They are the outward manifestations of our inner transformation, reflecting God's love and grace to a world in need of hope and healing. As we strive to embody kindness and compassion in our daily lives, may we be mindful of the ripple effect that our actions have on others, spreading positivity and light wherever we go. May we never underestimate the power of a simple act of kindness to make a difference in the lives of those around us, leaving a legacy of love and grace for generations to come.

Just as our bodies require
sustenance to thrive, our
souls also hunger for
nourishment – not for
physical food, but for
spiritual sustenance that
feeds our deepest
longings and desires.

Chapter 7: Filling Our Hunger

Just as our bodies require sustenance to thrive, our souls also hunger for nourishment—not for physical food, but for spiritual sustenance that feeds our deepest longings and desires. This hunger for righteousness, goodness, compassion, and love is an innate part of our human nature, driving us to seek fulfillment and meaning beyond the material world. In this chapter, we explore how we can fill this hunger and nourish our souls with the goodness of God.

At the core of filling our hunger for righteousness is the recognition that our souls crave connection with the divine. Just as physical hunger drives us to seek out food to satisfy our bodily needs, spiritual hunger compels us to seek out truth and goodness to satisfy our souls. This hunger is a reminder of our inherent desire for purpose and meaning, leading us on a journey of exploration and discovery as we seek to align our lives with God's will.

Prayer is one of the most powerful tools we have for filling our hunger for righteousness. Through prayer, we open ourselves up to God's presence and guidance, allowing his Spirit to work in and through us to transform our hearts and minds. As it says in Philippians 4:6–7, "Do not be anxious about anything, but in every situation, by prayer and petition, with thanksgiving, present your requests to God. And the peace of God, which transcends all understanding, will guard your hearts and your minds in Christ Jesus." Prayer is our direct line of communication with God, allowing us to express our deepest desires and concerns and to receive comfort, guidance, and strength in return.

Furthermore, fellowship with other believers is essential for filling our hunger for righteousness. As it says in Hebrews 10:24–25, "And let us consider how we may spur one another on toward love and good deeds, not giving up meeting together, as some are in the habit of doing, but encouraging one another—and all the more as you see the day approaching." When we gather with other believers, we are strengthened and encouraged in our faith, and we are reminded of the importance of living lives that reflect God's love and goodness. Fellowship allows us to share in each other's joys and sorrows, to support one another in times of need, and to hold each other accountable in our journey of discipleship.

Moreover, studying God's word is essential for filling our hunger for righteousness. As it says in 2 Timothy 3:16–17, "All Scripture is God-breathed and is useful for teaching, rebuking, correcting and training in righteousness, so that the servant of God may be thoroughly equipped for every good work." When we immerse ourselves in the Bible, we gain wisdom, insight, and understanding that guide us in living lives that honor God. The Bible serves as our roadmap for righteousness, providing us with the principles and precepts we need to navigate life's challenges and make choices that align with God's will.

Ultimately, filling our hunger for righteousness is about glorifying God through our actions. As it says in 1 Corinthians 10:31, "So whether you eat or drink or whatever you do, do it all for the glory of God." When we live lives that reflect God's love, goodness, and compassion, we bring honor and glory to his name. Our actions become a testimony to the transformative power of God's grace, inspiring others to seek him and to live lives that are pleasing to him.

Filling our hunger for righteousness is a lifelong journey that requires intentionality, discipline, and a willingness to seek God with our whole hearts. Through prayer, fellowship, and studying God's word, we deepen our connection with God and nourish our souls with the goodness of his love. And as we live lives that reflect God's love and goodness, we bring honor and glory to his name, fulfilling our purpose as his disciples in the world. May we continue to seek after righteousness with all our hearts, minds, and souls, knowing that in God alone can we find true fulfillment and satisfaction.

Kindness has the
remarkable ability to
brighten someone's day, lift
their spirits, and restore
their faith in humanity.

Chapter 8: Illuminating the Path Forward

As we ponder our roles as Salt and Light in this world, it's essential to translate these concepts into actionable steps in our daily lives. Each of us has the power to make a difference, whether through simple acts of kindness, compassion or by spreading positivity. In this chapter, we'll explore how we can embody the principles of Salt and Light and illuminate a path of hope and love for others to follow.

One of the most powerful ways we can embody the concept of Salt and Light is through acts of kindness. Kindness has the remarkable ability to brighten someone's day, lift their spirits, and restore their faith in humanity. Whether it's offering a helping hand to a neighbor in need, lending a listening ear to a friend going through a tough time, or simply offering a smile to a stranger, acts of kindness have a ripple effect that spreads far and wide. As it says in Ephesians 4:32, "Be kind and compassionate to one another, forgiving each other, just as in Christ God forgave you." By extending kindness to others, we reflect the love and compassion of Christ and illuminate the path of hope and love for others to follow.

Moreover, compassion is another essential aspect of embodying the principles of Salt and Light. Compassion involves putting ourselves in the shoes of others, empathizing with their struggles, and taking action to alleviate their suffering. As it says in Colossians 3:12, "Therefore, as God's chosen people, holy and dearly loved, clothe yourselves with compassion, kindness, humility, gentleness, and patience." When we show compassion to others, we demonstrate the love of Christ and become beacons of hope and healing in a world that desperately needs it.

Furthermore, spreading positivity is a powerful way to embody the principles of Salt and Light. In a world filled with negativity and despair, our words and actions have the power to uplift, encourage, and inspire others. Whether it's offering words of encouragement to a friend facing a difficult situation, sharing an inspiring story on social media, or simply choosing to see the good in others, spreading positivity can have a profound impact on those around us. As it says in Proverbs 16:24, "Gracious words are a honeycomb, sweet to the soul and healing to the bones." By spreading positivity, we bring light into the darkness and illuminate a path of hope and love for others to follow.

Together, let's commit to shining brightly as Salt and Light in our communities. Let's be intentional about extending kindness, showing compassion, and spreading positivity wherever we go. By embodying these principles in our daily lives, we can make a difference in the lives of those around us and be agents of transformation in a world that desperately needs it. As Matthew 5:16 says, "In the same way, let your light shine before others, that they may see your good deeds and glorify your Father in heaven." Let's illuminate the path forward with hope, love, and the transformative power of Christ's love.

Forgiveness is an integral aspect of the Christian faith, rooted in the teachings and example of Jesus Christ.

Chapter 9: Forgiveness—The Essence of Salt and Light

In a world often marred by conflict, resentment, and strife, forgiveness stands as a beacon of hope, illuminating the path to reconciliation and healing. As we explore the profound connection between forgiveness and the roles of Salt and Light, we uncover the transformative power of extending grace and mercy to others.

Forgiveness is an integral aspect of the Christian faith, rooted in the teachings and example of Jesus Christ. His life was a testament to the transformative power of forgiveness, as he extended grace and mercy to all, regardless of their shortcomings or transgressions. In the Gospels, we find numerous instances where Jesus demonstrated the profound impact of forgiveness, both through his words and actions.

One of the most poignant examples of forgiveness in the life of Jesus is found in the story of the woman caught in adultery (John 8:1–11). Confronted by the religious leaders, who sought to condemn her to death by stoning, Jesus responded with compassion and grace. He challenged the accusers, inviting them to reflect on their sins before casting judgment on others. Then, turning to the woman, he offered her forgiveness and a new beginning, urging her to go and sin no more.

In this encounter, Jesus exemplified the essence of Salt and Light through his willingness to forgive, even in the face of condemnation and judgment. His actions not only restored dignity and worth to the woman but also served as a powerful reminder of the transformative power of forgiveness in healing brokenness and restoring relationships.

Similarly, the parable of the prodigal son (Luke 15:11–32) illustrates the profound depth of God's forgiveness and the joy that comes from reconciliation. Despite squandering his inheritance and living a life of rebellion, the prodigal son is welcomed back with open arms by his father, who embraces him with love and forgiveness. Through this parable, Jesus teaches us about the boundless nature of God's mercy and the transformative impact of forgiveness in restoring broken relationships.

As followers of Christ, we are called to embody the spirit of forgiveness in our own lives, serving as agents of reconciliation and healing in a broken world. Just as salt enhances flavor and light dispels darkness, forgiveness has the power to bring healing and restoration to even the most broken of relationships.

Forgiveness is not easy, nor is it a sign of weakness. It requires humility, courage, and a willingness to let go of anger, resentment, and bitterness. However, the rewards of forgiveness far outweigh the challenges, as it frees us from the burden of carrying grudges and allows us to experience the transformative power of God's love in our lives.

Moreover, forgiveness is not just about letting go of past hurts; it is also about extending grace and mercy to others, just as God has extended grace and mercy to us. In the Lord's Prayer, Jesus teaches us to pray, "Forgive us our trespasses, as we forgive those who trespass against us." This prayer reminds us of the inseparable connection between receiving God's forgiveness and extending forgiveness to others.

Indeed, forgiveness is a fundamental aspect of our identity as followers of Christ, reflecting the essence of Salt and Light in a world hungering for reconciliation and healing. As we extend grace and mercy to others, we become agents of transformation, illuminating the darkness with the radiant light of God's love.

Forgiveness is indeed salt and light in a world thirsting for reconciliation and healing. Through the example of Jesus Christ and his teachings, we discover the transformative power of forgiveness in restoring broken relationships and healing wounded hearts. As we embody the spirit of forgiveness in our own lives, we become agents of reconciliation and healing, shining brightly as Salt and Light in a world hungering for grace and mercy.

In a world often clouded
by deception, dishonesty,
and falsehoods, honesty
is a cornerstone of
integrity, illuminating the
path to authenticity and
trustworthiness.

Chapter 10: Honesty—The Pillar of Salt and Light

In a world often clouded by deception, dishonesty, and falsehoods, honesty stands as a cornerstone of integrity, illuminating the path to authenticity and trustworthiness. As we explore the profound connection between honesty and the roles of Salt and Light, we uncover the transformative power of living with integrity and truthfulness.

Honesty is a fundamental virtue within the Christian faith, deeply rooted in the teachings and example of Jesus Christ. Throughout his ministry, Jesus emphasized the importance of truthfulness and integrity, urging his followers to speak and act with sincerity and honesty. In the Gospels, we find numerous instances where Jesus demonstrated the transformative impact of honesty, both through his words and his actions.

One of the most notable examples of honesty in the life of Jesus is found in his interactions with the Pharisees and religious leaders. Despite their attempts to deceive and trap him with their questions, Jesus responded with clarity and truthfulness, exposing their hypocrisy and falsehoods. His unwavering commitment to honesty served as a powerful example for his disciples and continues to inspire believers today.

Moreover, Jesus himself declared, "I am the way, the truth, and the life" (John 14:6), underscoring the intrinsic connection between truthfulness and the Christian faith. As followers of Christ, we are called to embody his example of honesty in our own lives, serving as beacons of truth and integrity in a world often plagued by deception.

The Apostle Paul also emphasized the importance of honesty in his letters to the early Christian communities. In Ephesians 4:25, he writes, "Therefore each of you must put off falsehood and speak truthfully to your neighbor, for we are all members of one body." Paul recognized that honesty is not merely a personal virtue but a communal responsibility, essential for fostering unity and trust within the body of Christ.

Furthermore, honesty is closely intertwined with the roles of Salt and Light described by Jesus in the Sermon on the Mount. Salt, as a preserving agent, prevents decay and corruption, while light exposes the darkness and reveals the truth. Similarly, honesty serves to preserve moral integrity and expose falsehoods, thereby fulfilling the roles of Salt and Light in a world hungering for authenticity and transparency.

Living with honesty requires courage, humility, and a commitment to moral integrity. It means speaking the truth even when it is uncomfortable or inconvenient and admitting our mistakes and shortcomings with sincerity and humility. However, the rewards of honesty far outweigh the challenges, as it fosters trust, builds relationships, and promotes accountability in both personal and communal settings.

Moreover, honesty is not just about verbal communication; it also encompasses honesty in our actions, intentions, and motives. It means living with integrity and authenticity, aligning our words and deeds with the values and principles of the Gospel. In this way, honesty becomes a tangible expression of our faith, reflecting the transformative power of God's truth in our lives.

As followers of Christ, we are called to be salt and light in a world hungering for authenticity and transparency. This requires a commitment to honesty in all aspects of our lives, serving as beacons of truth and integrity in a world often clouded by deception and falsehoods. By embodying the virtues of honesty, we fulfill our roles as salt and light, preserving moral integrity and illuminating the path to righteousness for all.

Honesty is indeed a pillar of Salt and Light in a world hungering for authenticity and transparency. Through the teachings and example of Jesus Christ, we discover the transformative power of honesty in fostering trust, building relationships, and promoting accountability. As followers of Christ, may we embody the virtue of honesty in our words and deeds, serving as beacons of truth and integrity in a world often clouded by deception and falsehoods.

trust is fragile and
vulnerable to erosion
through deceit, betrayal,
and hypocrisy.

Chapter 11: Trust in Salt and Light—A Deep Dive into Faith, Integrity, and Influence

The metaphors of salt and light have transcended time, becoming emblematic of Christian values and principles. Yet, beyond their spiritual connotations, they encapsulate profound truths about trust, integrity, and influence. This Chapter delves into the intricate relationship between trust and the symbolism of salt and light in the context of the Christian faith, exploring their implications for individuals and communities.

Trust forms the bedrock of human relationships, underpinning social cohesion and cooperation. It is a multifaceted concept, encompassing reliability, integrity, and confidence in others. Trust is earned through consistent behavior, honesty, and transparency, fostering a sense of security and mutual respect. In religious contexts, trust extends beyond human interactions to encompass faith in divine providence and spiritual guidance. The concept of trust serves as a lens through which to examine the significance of salt and light in Christian theology.

The effectiveness of salt as a preservative hinges on its purity and integrity. Similarly, trust is contingent upon the consistency and sincerity of one's actions. The ethical dimension of trust demands adherence to moral principles and a commitment to righteousness. In the Christian ethos, integrity is inseparable from faithfulness to God's Commandments and the teachings of Christ. The salt metaphor thus underscores the importance of moral integrity in earning and maintaining trust within communities.

Salt not only preserves but also permeates and transforms its surroundings. Likewise, trust empowers individuals to exert a positive influence on their environment. Through acts of kindness, compassion, and justice, believers can effectuate meaningful change in society. The metaphorical imagery of salt reminds Christians of their duty to be agents of transformation, combating moral decay and illuminating the path to righteousness.

Despite its intrinsic value, salt can lose its effectiveness if contaminated or diluted. Similarly, trust is fragile and vulnerable to erosion through deceit, betrayal, and hypocrisy. The challenges to trustworthiness are manifold, ranging from personal temptations to systemic injustices. In the pursuit of integrity, Christians confront internal struggles and external pressures that test their commitment to ethical principles. Overcoming these challenges requires vigilance, humility, and a steadfast reliance on divine grace.

Light exposes hidden truths and shadows of doubt and fear. Similarly, trust thrives in an environment of transparency, honesty, and openness. The virtue of honesty is paramount in fostering authentic relationships and building credibility. Christians are called to emulate the transparency of light in their interactions, eschewing falsehood and deceit. Through genuine sincerity and vulnerability, they cultivate trust and promote a culture of accountability and integrity.

Light not only reveals but also guides and inspires. It illuminates the way forward, dispelling confusion and instilling hope. Likewise, trust empowers individuals to serve as beacons of guidance and inspiration to others. Through their words and deeds, believers can shine a light on the darkness of ignorance, injustice, and despair. The metaphorical imagery of light underscores the transformative power of trust in fostering collective enlightenment and spiritual awakening.

In a world fraught with moral ambiguity and ethical dilemmas, trust serves as a moral compass, guiding individuals through uncertain terrain. The moral clarity of trust enables believers to discern right from wrong and uphold their convictions with unwavering resolve. However, navigating moral complexity requires discernment, humility, and a willingness to grapple with ambiguity. Christians are called to exercise prudence and wisdom in their decision-making, seeking guidance from divine wisdom and moral principles.

Trust is the cornerstone of vibrant and resilient communities. It fosters cooperation, empathy, and solidarity, binding individuals together in a shared pursuit of common goals. In Christian communities, trust forms the basis of fellowship and mutual support, transcending differences of race, culture, and background. Cultivating trustworthy communities requires intentional efforts to foster inclusivity, accountability, and reconciliation. By nurturing an ethos of trust and collaboration, Christians can build resilient communities that embody the values of justice, compassion, and love.

In the profound symbolism of salt and light, Christians find a compelling vision of trust, integrity, and influence. As "the salt of the earth" and "the light of the world," believers are called to embody these virtues in their daily lives, serving as agents of transformation and beacons of hope in a world hungering for authenticity and truth. In the crucible of trust, Christians discover the transformative power of faith, integrity, and compassion, illuminating the path to a more just, compassionate, and resilient society.

As we embark on this journey, may we be empowered by the transformative power of courage and righteousness to be salt and light in a world hungering for justice and truth.

Chapter 12: Courageous and Righteous—Becoming Biblical Salt and Light

In the preceding chapters, we have explored the profound symbolism of salt and light in the teachings of Jesus Christ. We have delved into the transformative power of trust, integrity, and influence, and uncovered the profound implications of these virtues for our lives and communities. Now, as we conclude our journey, we turn our attention to the imperative of embodying courage and righteousness as biblical salt and light.

Courage is a virtue that lies at the heart of the Christian faith. It is the willingness to stand firm in the face of adversity, to speak truth to power, and to defend the marginalized and oppressed. In the Bible, we find countless examples of courage, from the bravery of David facing Goliath to the steadfastness of Esther risking her life to save her people. As followers of Christ, we are called to emulate their courage, to be bold and unwavering in our commitment to righteousness and justice.

Righteousness is another cornerstone of the Christian ethos. It is the moral integrity that stems from a deep-seated commitment to God's commandments and the teachings of Christ. In a world rife with moral ambiguity and ethical compromise, righteousness serves as a guiding light, illuminating the path to truth and goodness. As salt and light in a dark and decaying world, we are called to embody righteousness in all aspects of our lives, to be beacons of moral clarity and integrity.

As the salt of the earth, we are called to preserve and transform society through our courageous witness. This requires the willingness to confront injustice and oppression, even at great personal cost. like salt that flavors and preserves, our courage infuses the world with the transformative power of justice and compassion. Whether it be advocating for the marginalized, speaking out against corruption, or challenging systems of oppression, our courage as salt empowers us to make a tangible difference in the world around us.

As the light of the world, we are called to illuminate the darkness with the radiance of God's truth and goodness. This requires an unwavering commitment to righteousness, even in the face of moral relativism and compromise. Like a beacon shining in the night, our righteousness dispels the shadows of falsehood and deception, revealing the path to spiritual enlightenment and salvation. Whether it be through acts of compassion, kindness, or forgiveness, our righteousness as light illuminates the world with the transformative power of God's love.

Courage and righteousness are not abstract ideals but lived realities that find expression in our daily lives. They compel us to act as agents of change and transformation in our communities. Whether it be through advocacy, activism, or service, our courageous and righteous deeds have the power to inspire others and effect lasting change. As salt and light in a world hungering for justice and truth, we are called to embody the transformative power of courage and righteousness in all that we do.

The journey of becoming biblical salt and light requires us to embrace the call to courage and righteousness with unwavering resolve. It challenges us to stand firm in the face of adversity, to speak truth to power, and to defend the oppressed. It calls us to embody moral integrity and steadfast commitment to God's Commandments and the teachings of Christ. As we embark on this journey, may we be empowered by the transformative power of courage and righteousness to be salt and light in a world hungering for justice and truth.

As we continue to
walk in the footsteps
of Jesus, may we
remain steadfast in
our commitment to
live lives of integrity,
compassion, and
righteousness

Chapter 13: Prayer

As we reflect on the journey of faith and the call to be Salt and Light, let us delve into the profound significance of this metaphorical concept. It is not merely a theoretical or abstract idea, but rather a practical and transformative way of living that resonates deeply with the teachings of Jesus Christ. Our role as disciples of Christ extends beyond mere words or beliefs; it is vividly demonstrated through our actions, attitudes, and relationships.

In the Gospel of Matthew, Jesus declares to his disciples, "You are the salt of the earth. But if the salt loses its saltiness, how can it be made salty again? It is no longer good for anything, except to be thrown out and trampled underfoot" (Matthew 5:13). This metaphorical imagery of salt carries profound implications for our lives as followers of Christ. Salt serves as a preservative, enhances flavor, and symbolizes purity. Likewise, as Christians, we are called to preserve the values of the Kingdom of God, to bring flavor to the world through our actions, and to embody purity of heart and character.

Furthermore, Jesus proclaims, "You are the light of the world. A town built on a hill cannot be hidden. Neither do people light a lamp and put it under a bowl. Instead, they put it on its stand, and it gives light to everyone in the house. In the same way, let your light shine before others, that they may see your good deeds and glorify your Father in heaven" (Matthew 5:14–16). Here, Jesus employs the imagery of light to illustrate the transformative impact of our lives when we live following the principles of the Kingdom. As bearers of God's light, we are called to dispel darkness, illuminate the path for others, and reflect the radiance of God's love and grace.

As we continue to walk in the footsteps of Jesus, may we remain steadfast in our commitment to live lives of integrity, compassion, and righteousness. Let us never underestimate the profound impact of even the smallest acts of kindness, for through them, we can truly make a difference in the world around us. Whether it be offering a helping hand to the marginalized, extending forgiveness to the broken-hearted, or speaking out against injustice and oppression, let us embody the transformative power of Christ's love in every aspect of our lives.

In our pursuit of righteousness and our desire to shine as beacons of hope, let us draw strength and inspiration from the boundless love and grace of our Heavenly Father. May His Spirit empower us to overcome adversity, persevere in faith, and boldly proclaim the Good News to all who are willing to listen. Let us be unyielding in our commitment to embody the values of the Kingdom, to advocate for justice and peace, and to extend compassion and mercy to all those in need.

As we close this chapter and step into the next phase of our journey, let us carry with us the invaluable lessons learned, the profound friendships formed, and the cherished memories shared. May the light of Christ continue to guide our path, illuminating the way forward with hope, love, and the transformative power of his grace. Let us remain ever vigilant in our mission to be Salt and Light in a world hungering for truth and searching for meaning.

Together, let us go forth, Salt and Light in a world hungering for truth and searching for meaning. Let us be catalysts for positive change, ambassadors of reconciliation, and bearers of the message of salvation. For in doing so, we fulfill our purpose as disciples of Christ and bring glory to his name. As we bid farewell to this moment and embrace the adventures that lie ahead, may we do so with hearts full of gratitude, minds open to learning, and spirits attuned to the whispers of the Holy Spirit.

For in him, we find strength; in him, we find courage; and in him, we find everlasting hope. So let us go forth, dear friends, with joy and anticipation, knowing that our journey is not yet complete, but that each step we take brings us closer to the fulfillment of God's plan for our lives and the realization of his Kingdom here on earth. Amen.

Message from the Author

Embarking on the journey of writing a book is akin to embarking on a voyage of self-discovery. It is a process that demands introspection, vulnerability, and a willingness to confront one's deepest beliefs and convictions. As I reflect on the writing journey of Salt and Light, I am reminded of the profound transformation that unfolded within me—a transformation that I earnestly hope will similarly resonate with readers.

At the outset, the concept of Salt and Light captivated my imagination, drawing me into a realm of profound symbolism and spiritual depth. The metaphors of salt and light, as elucidated in the teachings of Jesus Christ, intrigued me with their timeless relevance and universal significance. Yet, as I delved deeper into the subject matter, I soon realized that this endeavor would be more than a mere exploration of theological concepts—it would be a personal odyssey of faith, integrity, and self-discovery.

As I grappled with the complexities of trust, integrity, and influence, I found myself confronting my own beliefs and strong feelings with renewed clarity and conviction. Each chapter became a crucible in which I examined the intricacies of these virtues, seeking to unravel their profound implications for my own life and the world around me. Through moments of introspection and contemplation, I uncovered new insights and perspectives that challenged my preconceived notions and expanded my understanding of faith and morality.

One of the most transformative aspects of the writing process was the cultivation of empathy and compassion. As I delved into the challenges of trustworthiness and the ethical dilemmas of our time, I found myself empathizing with the struggles of others and grappling with the complexities of human nature. Through storytelling and reflection, I sought to imbue the narrative with a sense of empathy and understanding, inviting readers to embark on a journey of self-discovery and moral reflection.

Moreover, the act of writing itself became a catalyst for personal growth and transformation. In the solitude of my writing desk, I confronted my fears, doubts, and insecurities with courage and resilience. Through the creative process, I discovered a newfound sense of purpose and meaning, as each word and sentence became a testament to my commitment to truth and authenticity.

Yet, perhaps the most profound transformation occurred within the pages of the manuscript itself. As I poured my heart and soul into the narrative, I witnessed the emergence of a new vision—a vision of hope, renewal, and transformation. With each chapter, I sought to inspire readers to embrace the transformative power of faith, integrity, and influence, inviting them to embark on their journey of self-discovery and spiritual growth.

As I pen these final words, my sincere hope is that this book about Salt and Light will resonate with readers in a profound and meaningful way. May it serve as a source of inspiration and guidance, empowering readers to embrace the transformative power of trust, integrity, and influence in their own lives. May it remind us all that, in the journey of self-discovery, the greatest transformation begins within the depths of our own hearts and minds.

About the Author

My upbringing was imbued with the values and teachings of biblical beliefs, shaping the canvas of my fondest childhood memories. My childhood instilled in me the values of community, neighborly love, and the significance of education, all rooted in biblical teachings. The diversity of lifestyles, from poverty to affluence, provided valuable lessons in empathy and understanding, echoing the biblical call to love one another as we love ourselves. While I refrain from sharing specific recollections, the echoes of biblical stories of resilience and faith resonate deeply, encapsulating the trials and triumphs of my upbringing. Attending church with my mother provided a spiritual foundation grounded in biblical truth. From the musky scent of the carpet to the preacher's impassioned sermons, the church became a sanctuary of biblical wisdom and fellowship. Within those cream-colored walls, I cultivated friendships, learned to play piano, and found solace in the choir's harmonies, all reflecting the biblical principles of community and worship. In these memories, I recognize the profound influence that my upbringing, deeply rooted in biblical beliefs, had in shaping the person I am today and igniting my passion for storytelling in ways that honor God's grace and truth.